COUNTRIES

CUBA

by Alicia Z. Klepeis

WWW.FOCUSREADERS.COM

Copyright © 2025 by Focus Readers®, Mendota Heights, MN 55120. All rights reserved. No part of this book may be reproduced or utilized in any form or by any means without written permission from the publisher.

Focus Readers is distributed by North Star Editions:
sales@northstareditions.com | 888-417-0195

Produced for Focus Readers by Red Line Editorial.

Content Consultant: Louis A. Pérez, PhD, Professor of History, University of North Carolina at Chapel Hill

Photographs ©: iStockphoto, cover, 1, 4–5, 16, 26–27; Red Line Editorial, 7; Maria Breuer/Mauritius Images GmbH/Alamy, 8–9; Library of Congress, 11; Shutterstock Images, 13, 14–15, 19, 20–21, 23, 25; Kobby Dagan/VWPics/AP Images, 28

Library of Congress Cataloging-in-Publication Data
Names: Klepeis, Alicia, 1971- author.
Title: Cuba / by Alicia Z. Klepeis.
Description: Mendota Heights, MN: Focus Readers, [2025] | Series: Countries | Includes index | Audience: Grades 4-6 Focus Readers
Identifiers: LCCN 2024035788 (print) | LCCN 2024035789 (ebook) | ISBN 9798889983323 ebook | ISBN 9798889983828 pdf | ISBN 9798889982760 paperback | ISBN 9798889982203 hardcover
Subjects: LCSH: Cuba--Juvenile literature.
Classification: LCC F1758.5 .K54 2025 (print) | LCC F1758.5 (ebook) | DDC 972.91--dc23/eng/20240808
LC record available at https://lccn.loc.gov/2024035788
LC ebook record available at https://lccn.loc.gov/2024035789

Printed in the United States of America
Mankato, MN
012025

ABOUT THE AUTHOR
Alicia Z. Klepeis began her career at the National Geographic Society. A former middle school teacher, she is the author of numerous children's books, including *Go Wild! Frogs* and *Secrets of the Forest: 15 Bedtime Stories Inspired by Nature*. Alicia loves bringing the world to young readers through her books and school visits.

TABLE OF CONTENTS

CHAPTER 1
Welcome to Cuba 5

CHAPTER 2
History 9

CHAPTER 3
Climate, Plants, and Animals 15

CLIMATE CRISIS IN CUBA
Storms and Water 18

CHAPTER 4
Resources, Economy, and Government 21

CHAPTER 5
People and Culture 27

Focus Questions • 30
Glossary • 31
To Learn More • 32
Index • 32

CHAPTER 1

WELCOME TO CUBA

Cuba is a country in the Caribbean. The country is an **archipelago**. It includes more than 4,000 islands. The country's northern and eastern parts touch the Atlantic Ocean. The Caribbean Sea lies to the south. The Gulf of Mexico is to the northwest.

▶ Cuba has about 3,570 miles (5,745 km) of shoreline.

Cuba's largest island is also called Cuba. Havana is on this island's northwestern coast. Havana is Cuba's capital and largest city. More than two million people live there. The city is famous for its major port and colonial buildings. Isla de la Juventud is Cuba's second-largest island.

In southeast Cuba, the Sierra Maestra mountains rise. This region also has the Cauto River. It is Cuba's longest river. Central Cuba has the Sierra del Escambray range. The west has the Guaniguanico range. The main island also has grassy plains. Many people farm on these lowland areas.

The shores of Isla de la Juventud are swampy. This island has many hilly sections. Palm and pine trees dot the hills. Across Cuba, white sand beaches attract many visitors. Cuba's beautiful landscapes and history make it a fascinating country.

MAP OF CUBA

CHAPTER 2

HISTORY

People have lived in Cuba for at least 6,000 years. The earliest people were hunters and gatherers. They fished and farmed in the area. Many **Indigenous** groups lived in Cuba. These included the Guanahatabey, Ciboney, and Taíno.

In 1492, Christopher Columbus landed in Cuba. He claimed the land for Spain.

Taíno people often lived in thatched huts. Huts used branches, grass, and leaves.

Spanish explorers founded a settlement at Baracoa in 1511. They enslaved many Native people. Within decades, diseases and harsh working conditions had killed most Taíno people.

   Spanish settlers wanted to make money in ranching and tobacco. In the late 1700s, the sugar business grew. Sugar plantations needed many workers. Over the next hundred years, Europeans brought more than 850,000 enslaved Africans to work on Cuban plantations. By 1860, nearly one-third of the world's sugar came from Cuba.

   Many people in Cuba were unhappy with Spanish rule. In 1868, Carlos Manuel

Plantations needed workers to harvest crops, mills to process the sugar, and railroad access to transport it.

de Céspedes took action. He called on Cubans to fight for independence. This launched the Ten Years' War. Cuba did not win the war. But Spain promised to make reforms. Cubans were allowed to send representatives to Spain's government. In 1886, slavery finally ended in Cuba.

Over the years, tension continued between Cuba and Spain. Cubans tried several times to fight for independence. The War of Independence broke out in 1895. In 1898, the United States joined Cubans in a war against Spain. The Treaty of Paris granted Cuban independence from Spain. But US military forces stayed. The United States ruled Cuba until 1902.

Cuba's government changed many times during the early 1900s. **Corruption** and **dictatorship** were common problems. American influence was another. The United States often tried to support or overthrow Cuban leaders. In 1959, a young lawyer named Fidel Castro seized

Fidel Castro led Cuba from 1959 to 2008.

power. He declared Cuba a **Communist** state in 1961. Other Communist nations supported Cuba. But conflict with the United States continued. In the 2010s, Cuba's relationships with some foreign nations improved. Cuban people hoped for a brighter future.

CHAPTER 3
CLIMATE, PLANTS, AND ANIMALS

Cuba has a tropical climate. That means it is warm all year long. Wind patterns influence Cuba's rainfall. November to April is the dry season. May to October is the rainy season. Hurricanes usually hit between June and November.

A huge variety of plants live in Cuba. The butterfly lily is one example. It is

The Viñales valley contains a great variety of wildlife thanks to Cuba's warm climate.

Cuban trogons are Cuba's national bird. They are found only in Cuba.

Cuba's national flower. Forests cover nearly one-third of Cuba's land. Eastern Cuba has rainforests. Other areas have large tropical trees such as kapoks and palm trees. These trees thrive in Cuba's warm weather.

Many kinds of wildlife live across Cuba's habitats. Jellyfish float and glide among the coastal plants. Manatees swim in the waters. The rainforests are full of insects and birds. Rodents such as hutias are common, too.

The Zapata Swamp is in southwest Cuba. This swamp has animals that cannot be found anywhere else in the world. Rare crocodiles live there. Zapata wrens fly and feed on bugs.

COLORFUL CORAL REEFS

Many creatures swim in Cuba's colorful coral reefs. Some reefs are in the Jardines de la Reina archipelago. These reefs are famous for their beauty. Caribbean reef sharks swim there. The sharks hunt fish and squid. Goliath groupers live there, too. These huge fish can reach 800 pounds (360 kg).

CLIMATE CRISIS IN CUBA

STORMS AND WATER

Climate change is harming Cuba in many ways. For example, climate change often makes storms stronger. In 2022, Hurricane Ian hit western Cuba. The storm destroyed thousands of homes. It also ruined farm crops.

Climate change is causing other problems, too. Rising temperatures make rainy seasons longer. Farmers struggle with the extra rain. Their fields often flood. Crops may rot in the water. However, warmer temperatures can sometimes lead to too little water. Heat makes more water **evaporate**. That can cause longer periods without rain. More and more Cubans are struggling with these water shortages.

Sea levels are also rising due to climate change. This harms people and wildlife. The rising

Large waves may crash over Havana's seawall during storms.

water floods homes and buildings. It can also wipe out beaches. Plants that live near the coasts might lose their habitats, too.

Climate change also makes ocean waters warmer. That harms Cuba's coral reefs. Corals lose more **algae** in the heat. That can make the corals turn white and die. Coral death affects other species in the reef. People working in fishing and tourism may lose money, too.

CHAPTER 4

RESOURCES, ECONOMY, AND GOVERNMENT

Cuba has a variety of natural resources. The country has a larger source of nickel than most other nations in the world. That material is used to make stainless steel. It is also used for rechargeable batteries. Many other metals are found throughout Cuba. Iron and copper are two examples.

Nickel mining can cause pollution in rivers, leading to red water.

Oil is another valuable resource in Cuba. The country produces about half of the oil it needs. But turning the oil into gasoline can be difficult. In 2023, for example, fuel shortages were a problem in Cuba. So, Cuba planned to increase its supply of natural gas. It aimed to use more wind and solar power, too.

Farming is a key part of Cuba's economy. Coffee, fruits, and vegetables are important crops. So are sugarcane and tobacco. Some factories in Cuba turn sugarcane into molasses and rum. Others use tobacco to make cigars and cigarettes. Many of these products are shipped off. They go to countries all over

Producing Cuban cigars requires growing a lot of tobacco.

the world. Cuban factories produce many other goods, too. Medicines, steel, and cement are just a few.

Several other industries are important in Cuba. Many Cubans work in service industries. Education and health care employ many people. The tourist industry has expanded, too.

Cuba is a **socialist** country. The Communist Party is Cuba's only legal political party. The government controls or influences many parts of daily life. It also limits access to some information and media. Punishments are harsh for people who act against the government.

US SANCTIONS

In 1962, the United States placed **sanctions** on Cuba. US leaders hoped this would hurt Cuba's economy and weaken its government. Because of the sanctions, many Cubans struggled. It became harder to get food and medicine. Over time, some sanctions lessened. Cubans in the United States could send some money to family back home. Travel to Cuba became easier, too.

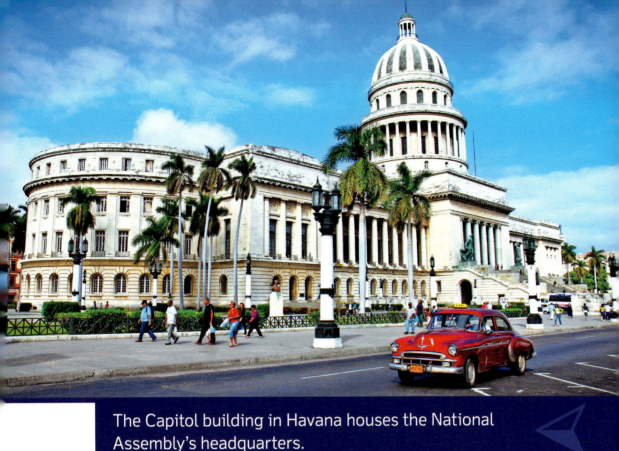

The Capitol building in Havana houses the National Assembly's headquarters.

Cuba's government includes the National Assembly of People's Power. This group makes Cuba's laws. It also picks Cuba's president. The president chooses a prime minister and other officials. The government also includes a Supreme Court.

CHAPTER 5

PEOPLE AND CULTURE

More than 11 million people live in Cuba. Most Cubans speak Spanish. That is Cuba's official language. Some Cubans speak English as well.

Religion is important to many Cubans. More than half the population is Christian. Most people are Catholic. Some are Protestant. Santería is another

Camagüey is the largest inland city in Cuba. Many of its historic buildings are still standing.

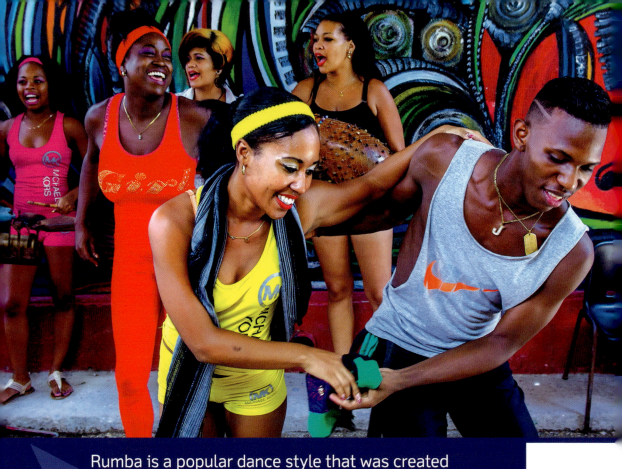

Rumba is a popular dance style that was created in Cuba.

common religion. Santería combines Catholic and West African traditions.

Music is another important part of Cuban culture. Cuban folk music blends Spanish and African influences. Salsa is a common musical style. Salsa combines jazz with traditional instruments and rhythms. Modern music genres are popular, too. Rap is one example.

Sports are a favorite pastime for many Cubans. Baseball is the nation's most popular sport. Cuba's baseball team has won three Olympic gold medals. Soccer is another huge sport. These pastimes all help make up Cuba's rich culture.

FILM IN CUBA

Cuba has an active film industry. Some Cuban filmmakers create movies to share their culture. Their films entertain people all over the world. Filmmakers from other countries also go to Cuba. The country is a popular filming site. For example, parts of *The Fate of the Furious* were filmed in Havana.

FOCUS QUESTIONS

Write your answers on a separate piece of paper.

1. Write a paragraph describing the main ideas of Chapter 4.

2. What are some similarities between Cuba and the country you live in? What are some differences?

3. When did Fidel Castro seize power in Cuba?
    - **A.** 1938
    - **B.** 1959
    - **C.** 1982

4. What might happen if a Cuban citizen tried to start a new political party?
    - **A.** They might be encouraged to gather support.
    - **B.** They might be asked to join the government.
    - **C.** They might be punished by the government.

Answer key on page 32.

GLOSSARY

algae
Tiny plant-like organisms that produce oxygen.

archipelago
A group of islands.

climate change
A human-caused global crisis involving long-term changes in Earth's temperature and weather patterns.

Communist
Having to do with a political system in which all property is owned by the public.

corruption
Dishonest or illegal acts, especially by powerful people.

dictatorship
A form of government in which one leader has full power.

evaporate
To change from a liquid to a gas.

Indigenous
Native to a region.

sanctions
Penalties meant to force a country to change its behavior.

socialist
Having a political system in which the government controls resources to promote equality.

TO LEARN MORE

BOOKS

Banks, Rosie. *Celebrating the People of Cuba*. New York: Cavendish Square Publishing, 2023.

Hudak, Heather C. *Focus on Cuba*. New York: Crabtree Publishing, 2024.

Van, R. L. *Cuba*. Minneapolis: Abdo Publishing, 2023.

NOTE TO EDUCATORS

Visit **www.focusreaders.com** to find lesson plans, activities, links, and other resources related to this title.

INDEX

Castro, Fidel, 12
climate change, 18–19
Columbus, Christopher, 9
Communist, 13, 24–25
culture, 28–29

economy, 22, 24

factories, 22–23
farming, 6, 9, 18, 22

government, 11–12, 24–25

Havana, 6–7, 29

independence, 11–12
Indigenous groups, 9
Isla de la Juventud, 6–7

languages, 27

plantations, 10
plants, 15–16, 19

religions, 27–28

slavery, 10–11
Spain, 9, 11–12

United States, 7, 12–13, 24

wildlife, 16, 18

Answer Key: 1. Answers will vary; 2. Answers will vary; 3. B; 4. C